READER'S DIGEST

POCKET GUIDE TO

Herbs

D1440092

The Reader's Digest Association Limited

London

The Publishers wish to express their gratitude to
the following people who have contributed to and advised on
the preparation of this guide:

Text
KENNETH A. BECKETT
TOM STOBART, O.B.E.
Illustrations
ELSIE WRIGLEY, A.T.D., D.A. (MAN.)

Further information on herbs, as well as a
glossary of botanical and horticultural terms, will be found in

THE READER'S DIGEST
ENCYCLOPAEDIA OF GARDEN
PLANTS AND FLOWERS

Contents

4 Introduction

6 Cultivation

15 The herb garden

39 The use of herbs

45 Recipes

Introduction

BOTANICALLY, a herb is any plant whose stems die down completely in winter. In common usage, the term is applied to aromatic plants whose leaves, stems, flowers or seeds have culinary or medicinal uses.

Records show that herbs were in use in ancient Greece; they were valued as flavourings and for their fragrance, and they also formed the basis of medical treatment. Hippocrates, the Greek physician (*c.* 460 BC), listed several hundred herbal remedies whose use persisted for many centuries. The ancient world also credited certain herbs with mystical properties.

Herbs were introduced into Britain by the Romans, who adopted many of the Greek customs. They, too, valued the reputedly supernatural powers of the plants, as well as their culinary and medicinal uses. The wreath of bay laurel worn by victors of wars, games and contests is well known. In Britain, too, herbs became a focus of superstition, reaching their peak of importance in the Middle Ages when every village had its witch, and every witch her herbs and potions. Herbs were also used to counteract the witches' powers; garlic, hyssop and wormwood all combated witchcraft and evil spirits. Even today, in remote country districts of Romania, doorposts are festooned with wreaths of garlic, to ward off vampires! The Christian Church also used herbs in rites and ceremonies, and every cathedral and monastery had its herb garden.

The medicinal qualities of herbs were even more important. In 1597, John Gerard, the London herbalist and apothecary, published his *Herball*, a volume weighing 10 lb. and containing 1000 pages with woodcut illustrations of 3000 plants. Herbal remedies continued to be the main preoccupation of physicians until the 18th century, and even today, certain drugs are still obtained from natural sources. The pain-killing drug morphine is derived from poppies; digitalin, a heart stimulant, is extracted from foxgloves; and colchicine, used in the treatment of rheumatic conditions, is obtained from the autumn crocus (*Colchicum*).

The culinary use of herbs reached its climax during the 16th century. This was the age of the Elizabethan herb garden; a well-stocked garden would have up to 60 different herbs, for use in medicinal drinks, for scents and for cooking. These gardens were laid out in decorative, often intricate, patterns interspersed with low-growing hedges of lavender, rosemary or box.

During the 19th century the cultivation and use of herbs began to decline. At the beginning of the 20th century, the herbs commonly used had been reduced to four: mint, parsley, sage and thyme. However, with the rising popularity of highly flavoured dishes, attention is once more focused on the herb garden.

Cultivation

ALTHOUGH many herbs, particularly perennials and sub-shrubs, are often grown in mixed herbaceous borders, herbs needed for the kitchen are best grown in a plot of their own. Where space is limited, a few choice plants can be grown in a window-box or in pots on a sunny window-sill. Where space allows, a selection that includes bay, borage, chives, fennel, mint, parsley, rosemary, sage, sorrel, savory, tarragon and thyme would be adequate for most kitchen gardens.

SOIL AND POSITION

Generally, herbs thrive on light, fertile and well-drained soil; but they do well in any ordinary, even poor, garden soil. With the exception of sorrel, all herbs thrive on alkaline soils and benefit from an annual fertiliser containing lime.

As most herbs originate in the warmer Mediterranean countries, they need a position in full sun. Ideally, the plot should be facing south and on a slight slope. Tall-growing, sun-loving species should be placed at the back of the plot, where they will not overshadow smaller plants. Angelica and parsley thrive in slightly moist soil.

In a small garden, the herb plot may be integrated with

the vegetable garden, although ideally it should be near the kitchen. Where space permits, there is wide scope for variation in the layout of a herb garden, to secure the most effective contrast of height, leaf-form and colour. A round bed can be marked in wedge-shaped segments around a central feature, such as a sundial, and each segment planted with a different herb.

Another attractive layout is the chessboard pattern. Alternate the squares of herbs with empty squares, either paved or filled with gravel or granite chippings; this permits easy access to each group of herbs.

Complicated designs, like those of the Elizabethan knot gardens, are impracticable for the average garden, but may be worth the trouble in large gardens. The individual beds, often of unequal size, are carefully planned to produce contrasting leaf textures and colours. The divisions between the beds may be planted with low hedges of box or with sweet-scented violets.

PREPARATION AND PLANTING
Prepare the site during winter by digging it to a spade's depth. Lighten heavy soil by digging in compost, peat or cold boiler ashes at the rate of 2 buckets per sq. yd.

In spring, rake the soil repeatedly until a fine tilth has been produced. Sow hardy annuals from March onwards, but delay sowing of half-hardy herbs until the danger of frost is over. The perennials may be planted in March and April or in September and October.

Sow seeds in drills, $\frac{1}{4}$–$\frac{1}{2}$ in. deep and 8–12 in. apart according to the eventual spread of the varieties. As soon as the seedlings are large enough to handle, thin them to stand 3 in. apart, later thinning to the final spacings.

Parsley is extremely slow to germinate, and may take four to six weeks to produce the first seedlings. Germination is hastened by soaking the seeds in water for 12 hours before sowing.

Perennial herbs may also be raised from seeds, sown in spring. The drills should preferably be made in a separate nursery bed. After thinning the seedlings, leave them to grow on in the nursery bed and transplant to permanent sites in autumn or the following spring.

PROPAGATION

All perennial herbs can be increased from existing stock, by cuttings or division. Shrubby and sub-shrubby plants, such as rosemary and thyme, are readily propagated by cuttings. In July or August, take 2–4 in. long cuttings of half-ripe side-shoots. Sever the side-shoots just below a joint with a sharp knife. Strip the lower leaves of the cuttings off before inserting them in equal parts (by volume) peat and sand in a cold frame.

When the cuttings have rooted, pot them up singly in 3 in. containers of John Innes potting compost No. 1, and overwinter in a frost-free frame or greenhouse. The following April or May, set the young plants out in their permanent growing positions.

Bay, lavender, mint, rosemary, sage and thyme can also be increased from 4–8 in. hardwood cuttings taken from late July to September. These cuttings can be inserted directly in a nursery bed in the open. They should be making strong new growth by the following spring when they can be transplanted to their final growing quarters.

Chives should be divided every three or four years, in spring or autumn. Lift the clumps and separate into small clusters of shoots, or divide existing plants into several larger pieces by pulling them apart. Replant the divisions 10–12 in. apart. Overgrown plants of fennel and sorrel may be divided in the same manner, although fennel is best increased from seeds.

The tough underground stems of mint are invasive and will spread beyond the area where they are wanted unless they are confined: sink slates or tiles vertically in the soil. If more plants are wanted, or if existing plants are getting straggly, dig up the clump, discard the hard, woody centre and cut the remainder into pieces each containing part of a rhizome.

MANAGEMENT OF THE HERB GARDEN

Keep the plot free of weeds, which compete with the herbs for light, moisture and nourishment. During dry spells in summer, water plants such as angelica and parsley, that thrive in moist soil, to maintain vigorous growth. Alternatively, apply a mulch of peat in spring; this conserves moisture in the soil and acts as a weed suppressant.

9

Shrubby plants, particularly lavender and rosemary, whether grown as isolated plants or as low hedges, should be kept within bounds by annual pruning. In March, remove any dead and weak growths from rosemary and shorten straggly shoots to maintain a shapely bush. If the plant is old and overgrown, cut back all shoots by up to half, in April or September.

Remove the faded flower spikes from lavender in late summer, and lightly trim the plants to shape. In spring, straggly plants may be cut hard back to encourage bushy growth from the base of the plants. When lavender is grown as a low informal hedge, it should be clipped to shape annually in March or April.

PESTS AND DISEASES

In general, few pests attack herbs, but maggots of the carrot fly may occasionally attack the roots and stems of parsley, making young plants wilt and collapse. These pests can normally be controlled by treating the seeds with HCH seed-dressing before sowing, or by watering a trichlorphon solution into the soil round the plants.

Maggots of celery fly may sometimes feed on the leaves of parsley, producing unsightly brown blotches. In severe attacks, the leaves shrivel and growth is checked. Prevent infestation by spraying or dusting the young plants with malathion, dimethoate or trichlorphon.

Few diseases affect herbs, but rusts may show in spring as yellow or red spore pustules on swollen leaves and stems of chives and mint. Pale spots later develop on the leaves, which fall. Rusts are difficult to control as they remain within the tissues. At the end of the season, dig up and destroy any severely infected plants.

White rot may attack the foliage of garlic, causing it to become yellow and die back. The roots generally rot, and the bulbs are covered at the base with a white fluffy fungal growth. The disease persists in the soil, and garlic should preferably be grown on a fresh site each year. Prevent attacks by dusting the planting sites with calomel or benomyl dusts before planting.

Leaf spot appears on the leaves of spindly parsley plants as small brown spots, gradually changing to white. Spray at the first sign with captan, maneb or zineb. Yellow, orange and red discolorations on the leaves are due to a virus disease; attacks are seldom serious.

The leaves and stems of young sage plants may become covered with a white powdery coating, due to grey mould or powdery mildew. Spray with dinocap, benomyl or thiophanate-methyl as soon as symptoms are observed and continue at 2-weekly intervals.

HARVESTING AND DRYING

The time of harvesting depends on the purpose for which the herbs are grown. Plants cultivated for their leaves and stems should be harvested in the young stage, before flowering, while herbs grown for their flowers should be picked when in full bloom. Herbs chiefly grown for their seeds are gathered in late summer when the seeds ripen and turn yellow or brown.

Choose a dry, still day for harvesting and gather the herbs after morning dew has vanished, but before the sun becomes hot. Handle the leafy shoots carefully to avoid bruising and subsequent loss of aroma, and remove entirely any damaged and discoloured leaves. Large leaves may be stripped from the stems, but small-leaved herbs are better dried whole. If the leaves are gritty and dirty, wash them gently in cool water.

If the herbs are wanted for drying, place them on flat containers such as cardboard boxes or trays covered with cheesecloth, keeping one kind of herb well apart from another to avoid the mingling of aromas. Place the containers in a dry, warm and airy place. An airing cupboard or the warming drawer of a cooker is suitable provided there is adequate ventilation.

Turn the herbs once a day, handling them carefully. Most herbs are ready for storing after four or five days or when they are brittle to the touch. Before storing the herbs, check that they are perfectly dry by keeping them in clear glass containers for a week. If moisture gathers on the inside of the jars, spread out the herbs on trays and leave them to dry for a few more days.

When dry, the leaves should be stripped from the stems, although small-leaved herbs, such as hyssop and thyme, keep their aroma better if stored whole and then crumbled before use. Discard all chaff and pack the leaves or sprigs into airtight containers. It is best to use opaque containers; if clear glass jars are used, keep them out of direct light. Seal and label the containers.

Alternatively, small-leaved herbs may be tied in small bunches and hung upside down in a cool airy place to dry. When brittle, strip the leaves from the stems and store in airtight, opaque containers.

Herbs with tender leaves, such as chervil and parsley, are generally unsuitable for drying, but can be preserved by freezing. After cutting and cleaning the leaves, blanch them for one minute in boiling water, then rinse under cold running water until thoroughly chilled. Drain the leaves, and place them in small polythene bags or foil in the freezer. When required for use in stews, soups or sauces, the frozen herbs may be added to the dish or chopped while partly frozen.

Cut the flower spikes of lavender just before they open fully; tie in small bundles and hang upside down in a cool airy place. When completely dry, strip the flowers off the stems and store in airtight containers. The dried flowers may be used in sachets for the linen cupboard or drawers, or mixed with other dried flowers to make pomanders or *pot-pourris*.

Herbs such as caraway and dill, which are chiefly grown for their seeds, are dried for storage in the same way as leaves. Pick the stems in late summer or early autumn when the seeds are ripe and yellow-brown. Place them on shallow trays, or tie them with their stems in small bunches. Leave to dry for about a week, turning occasionally. When dry, remove the seeds and store in the same way as for dried leaves.

POMANDERS AND POT-POURRIS

Apart from their culinary use, herbs may be used to make aromatic mixtures with dried petals of fragrant flowers. Lavender sachets are well known, and dried sprigs of lemon thyme, balm, bergamot, marjoram and rosemary mixed with verbena, geranium, cloves and rose petals, also give long-lasting fragrance in rooms, linen closets and cupboards.

Pomander balls are made by closely covering oranges, limes or lemons with whole cloves. Leave the clove-covered fruit to dry in a cool airy room for about a month, then roll the fruit in equal parts (by volume) orris root and a herb-and-spice mixture of cloves, nutmeg, cinnamon and rosemary, or any other fragrant mixture. Leave the fruit with the spices in a deep box for a week, then shake and tie with ribbon.

Pot-pourris can be made from various mixtures of dried flowers and herbs. A fragrant mixture could consist of rose petals, rose geranium leaves, lavender flowers and sprigs of rosemary. Mix the dried flowers and leaves with crushed whole cloves, cinnamon and allspice, and bind with a proprietary '*pot-pourri* maker'. Place the mixture in open bowls or containers of glass or china, to release their fragrance in rooms and cupboards.

The herb garden

Most common herbs are easily obtained as seeds from nurseries or seedsmen; rare plants, such as costmary and lovage, are generally available from herb nurseries.

In the following descriptions, the countries referred to denote the place of origin of the herb.

ANGELICA
(*Angelica archangelica. Umbelliferae*)
Europe, naturalised in Great Britain. Height 6–10 ft; spread 3 ft. A robust, well-branched biennial or short-lived perennial. The large, pale to mid-green leaves are divided into ovate lobed leaflets. Tiny green-yellow flowers are borne from July to August.

ANGELICA

The young green stems can be candied and used as decoration for cakes and trifles. Pick them before the flowers open. Young blanched shoots may also be used in salads. A few chopped leaves make an unusual musky-flavoured addition to stewed rhubarb and orange marmalade.

Cut the stems into 5 in. sections, place them in a pan and cover with boiling syrup. Place a layer of vine or spinach leaves on top and leave the mixture until the next day; drain and discard the vine leaves. Boil up the syrup, strain and pour over the angelica stems. Cover these with fresh leaves until the following day. Repeat this process once more until the stems are bright green; bottle in clear jars.

Angelica requires a moisture-retentive soil, enriched with well-decayed manure, leaf-mould or peat, in sun or partial shade. Sow the seeds in drills when ripe, during August, or in March. Thin out the seedlings, when large enough to handle, or transplant to permanent quarters, setting them about 15 in. apart.

ANISE, aniseed
(*Pimpinella anisum. Umbelliferae*)

ANISE

Greece. Height 18 in.; spread 9–12 in. An annual plant, similar in appearance to celery, but smaller and more slender, with deeply cut mid-green leaves. Loose flat clusters, 2 in. across, of yellow-white flowers appear in July.

This plant is grown for its seeds which need a good warm summer to ripen. Gather the seeds when ripe and use them dried for flavouring sweets and creams. On the Continent, anise seeds, with their sweet liquorice flavour, are used in cakes and breads, but are most frequently an important ingredient of liqueurs and cordials. They may be used sparingly to marinate fish used for bouillon or soups.

Sow the seeds during April, in well-drained fertile soil open to the sun. Thin the seedlings to stand 9–12 in. apart.

BALM, lemon balm
(*Melissa officinalis. Labiatae*)
Europe, including Great Britain. Height 2–4 ft; spread 12–18 in. A mint-like, hardy herbaceous perennial. It has ovate, bright mid-green leaves, slightly corrugated. Tubular white flowers, about $\frac{1}{2}$ in. long, are borne in clusters in the upper leaf axils from July to September. The plant has a strong lemon scent when bruised.

Use the young chopped leaves fresh in salads and in sauces accompanying fish. They may also be used fresh or dried with other herbs in omelettes. They give a refreshing taste to wine-cups and iced drinks in summer.

Balm tolerates light shade and thrives in any soil that is not waterlogged. Plant at any time from October to March. Propagate by dividing the clumps in autumn.

BALM

BASIL, sweet
(*Ocimum basilicum. Labiatae*)
Tropical Africa, Asia, Pacific Islands. Height 2–3 ft; spread 12 in. This erect, branched, half-hardy annual has sweetly

aromatic, pale to mid-green leaves that are oblong and toothed. Small, tubular, white flowers are borne in 6–9 in. terminal clusters in August.

The sweet, clove-scented leaves should be used when young. Basil can be used to flavour soups, such as turkey soup, and is delicious when shredded over a tomato salad or any dish containing tomatoes. It is a good ingredient for sauces with fish and chicken, and for omelettes, soufflés and herb butters.

BASIL

The leaves will keep fresh for a short while, packed in polythene bags in a refrigerator, and are also suitable for freezing. However, the leaves keep their flavour best when preserved in oil. Pack clean leaves into a jar and sprinkle with salt before adding another layer of leaves. Fill the jar with olive oil and seal. In a refrigerator the preserved leaves will keep fresh for several months.

Basil needs a sheltered sunny site and a well-drained fertile soil. Sow seeds under glass in pans, boxes or pots of John Innes seed compost during March at a temperature of 13–15°C (55–59°F). Prick out the seedlings, when large enough to handle, into boxes of John Innes potting compost No. 1, and plant out into permanent quarters in late May. Alternatively, sow in the open in mid-May.

BAY, bay laurel

(*Laurus nobilis. Lauraceae*)

S. Europe. Height and spread 10 ft or more. A hardy evergreen shrub or tree of bushy growth and pyramidal habit while young. The oblong, pointed, dark green leaves are sweetly aromatic when bruised. Tufts, about 1 in. across, of yellow-green petal-less flowers open at the ends of the shoots in April and May. In warm seasons, they are followed by black, cherry-like fruits.

Bay may be grown as unrestricted shrubby specimens or as standards in tubs and trimmed to shape two or three times during summer. The leaves are used, fresh or dried, for flavouring almost any dish, including fish, stews, sauces and milk puddings and custards. It is a traditional ingredient of the *bouquet garni*.

Plant bay in well-drained soil in a site sheltered from strong north and east winds, during September and October or March and April. Propagate by cuttings, 3–4 in. long, of lateral shoots, taken in August or September. Insert the cuttings in equal parts (by volume) peat and sand in a cold frame. Pot when rooted in 3½ in. pots of John Innes potting compost No. 1; pot on as necessary. The following October, line the young plants out in a nursery bed and grow on for one or two years.

BAY

BERGAMOT, bee balm, Oswego tea

(*Monarda didyma. Labiatae*)
Eastern U.S.A. Height and spread 2–3 ft. This erect hardy perennial has prominently squared stems and pale to mid-green, toothed, ovate leaves. Tubular, bright scarlet flowers, $1\frac{1}{4}$–$1\frac{3}{4}$ in. long, are borne in dense heads from June to September.

Use the aromatic leaves shredded fresh in salads and in herbal teas; dried, they are suitable for *pot-pourri*.

The plant thrives in any fertile, moisture-retentive soil, in sun or partial shade. Plant at any time between October and March, 9–12 in. apart. Propagate by dividing and replanting the rhizomes during March. Seeds may be sown in March or April, outdoors or in pots or pans of John Innes seed compost placed in a cold frame. Prick out the seedlings, when large enough to handle, into a nursery bed and plant out in permanent positions in October.

BERGAMOT

BORAGE

(*Borago officinalis. Boraginaceae*)
Europe, including Great Britain. Height and spread $1\frac{1}{2}$–3 ft. A hardy annual, with large, ovate, roughly hairy, hoary-green leaves, smelling of cucumber when

BORAGE

bruised. Nodding, sky-blue, starry flowers, $\frac{3}{4}$–1 in. across, are borne in large terminal clusters from June to September.

The flowers can be candied and used for cake decoration; the young leaves are refreshing in iced drinks, or may be used finely chopped in salads.

Any fertile, well-drained soil, open to the sun, is suitable for borage. Sow the seeds during September or April, thinning the seedlings, when the first true leaves are well developed, to 12 in. apart. Leaves can be picked about eight weeks later. Once the herb is introduced into a garden, self-sown seedlings can usually be relied upon to perpetuate the species.

CARAWAY
(*Carum carvi. Umbelliferae*)
Europe, eastwards to N. India. Height up to 3 ft; spread 9–12 in. This slender, branched annual has finely divided, somewhat fern-like, mid-green leaves. Flattened heads, $1\frac{1}{2}$–2 in. across, of tiny white flowers develop during June.

The young green leaves, much less pungent in taste than the seeds, may be finely chopped and used in soups and salads. The strongly flavoured seeds should be gathered in late summer, and dried and stored for use in cakes and bread. They are also much used in cheeses and

CARAWAY

cabbage dishes, and are an important ingredient of many continental liqueurs.

Grow in fertile, well-drained garden soil in a sunny position. Sow seeds in September or in March and April, thinning the seedlings to 12 in. apart as soon as they are large enough to handle.

CHAMOMILE

(*Anthemis nobilis,* syn. *Chamaemelum nobile. Compositae*)
Europe, including Great Britain. Height 6–9 in.; spread 12–15 in. This low-growing hardy perennial has finely cut, rich green, mossy foliage, sweetly aromatic when bruised. White, daisy-like flowers, 2 in. across, open from June to August.

Use the dried flowers in herbal teas.

Plant chamomile 12–18 in. apart in a sunny site during September and October or in March and April. Any well-drained soil is suitable. Propagate by division during March or April. Alternatively, sow seeds outdoors in April, thinning the seedlings when large enough to handle, or transplanting to their permanent sites.

CHERVIL

(*Anthriscus cerefolium. Umbelliferae*)
E. Europe, eastwards to Iran; naturalised in Great Britain. Height 18 in.; spread

12 in. An erect, branched, hardy biennial with sweetly aromatic, mid-green and fern-like leaves. Tiny white flowers are borne in flat, lacy heads, about 3 in. wide, and open from June to August.

The young leaves have a distinctive aroma, slightly reminiscent of parsley. They should be used fresh, in soups and sauces or for garnish, and are usual in *fines herbes* for omelettes.

Chervil needs a well-drained fertile soil in partial shade. Sow seeds at four to six-week intervals from March to August to provide a succession of young leaves. Pinch out the flowers as soon as they are noticed. Thin the seedlings to stand 12 in. apart. A winter supply of fresh leaves can be obtained by sowing seeds under glass at a temperature of 7–10°C (45–50°F) at intervals from October to February. Sow thinly in pans or boxes of John Innes seed compost and prick off, 2–3 in. apart each way, into boxes of John Innes potting compost No. 2.

CHERVIL

CHIVES
(*Allium schoenoprasum. Alliaceae*)
Northern Hemisphere. Height 6–10 in.; spread 9–12 in. A tufted, perennial, non-bulbous onion with slender, somewhat grassy, tubular mid-green leaves. Globular, rose-purple flower heads, 1 in.

CHIVES

across, appear in June and July, but these should be removed as soon as noticed, to promote further young leaves.

The fresh leaves impart a mild onion flavour to salads, egg and cheese dishes, and are used in the preparation of *sauce tartare* and in *fines herbes*.

Chives thrive in any well-drained soil, preferably in a sunny site, but also in partial shade. Plant during suitable weather at any time from September to April. Every three or four years, in September, divide and replant the clumps into portions containing half a dozen shoots.

CORIANDER
(Coriandrum sativum. Umbelliferae)
S. Europe. Height up to 18 in.; spread 6–9 in. This slender, sparsely branched hardy annual has pale to mid-green lobed basal leaves and finely cut stem leaves. Tiny, very pale purple flowers are borne in loose, clustered and flattened heads, about $1\frac{1}{2}$ in. across, during June and July.

Gather the seeds when ripe, in late summer, for use in the dried state in curries and chutneys, and sprinkled on cakes, bread, milk puddings and cream cheeses.

Sow seeds in April in a light, fertile, well-drained soil open to the sun. Thin the seedlings to 4–6 in. apart, when large enough to handle.

CORIANDER

COSTMARY, alecost

(*Chrysanthemum balsamita. Compositae*)
Asia. Height up to 3 ft; spread 15 in. A
clump-forming hardy perennial, aromatic
when bruised. The mid-green leaves are
elliptic with a heart-shaped base. White
tansy-like flowers, $\frac{1}{2}$–$\frac{3}{4}$ in. across, are
borne in flattened terminal clusters in
September and October.

The leaves, which retain their aromatic
flavour well when dried, may be used to
flavour soups, forcemeats and salads.

Costmary thrives in any ordinary, moisture-retentive soil, preferably in sun,
though it tolerates partial shade. Plant
12–15 in. apart from September to March.
Propagate by division in September or
March. Replant immediately.

COSTMARY

DILL

(*Peucedanum graveolens. Umbelliferae*)
Europe. Height up to 3 ft; spread 9–12
in. This herb is a slender, erect, hardy
annual, resembling fennel in appearance.
The rich green leaves are divided into
narrow segments. From June to August,
tiny dull yellow flowers are borne in 2–3
in. wide, flattened heads.

Both leaves and dried seeds are used in
cooking. The decorative leaves are suitable
for garnishes, and also impart a distinctive aniseed flavour to salads, fish and

DILL

sauces. Leaves and dried seeds are used to flavour vinegars.

Dill requires a moisture-retentive but well-drained soil in a sunny site. Sow the seeds in March or April, thinning the seedlings, when large enough to handle, 9–12 in. apart.

FENNEL
(*Foeniculum vulgare. Umbelliferae*)
Europe. Height 5–8 ft; spread 24 in. A clump-forming hardy perennial with erect, much-branched stems. The sweetly aromatic, blue-green leaves consist of thread-like segments. Numerous 3–4 in. wide heads of yellow flowers open in July.

Use the leaves, fresh or dried, for herbal teas and for flavouring sauces accompanying fish. The slight aniseed flavour goes well with pork and veal; used sparingly, the finely chopped fresh leaves may be added to soups and vinaigrette sauces. The seeds are strongly flavoured and can be used to flavour pickled gherkins and cucumbers.

A sunny site is the most suitable, although light shade is tolerated. Sow seeds during March in any well-drained soil and thin the small seedlings to 24 in. apart. Fennel can be divided in March or April, but divisions are slow to become established and lack the vigour of seedlings.

FENNEL

GARLIC

(Allium sativum. Alliaceae)
Possibly E. Europe; extensively cultivated
throughout the world. Height (in flower)
1–3 ft; spread 9–12 in. This hardy,
onion-like perennial has grassy grey-
green leaves. During June, spherical heads
of white or purple-tinged starry flowers
appear; these should be removed in the
bud stage, to encourage the production of
large bulbs.

GARLIC

The bulb is composed of a number of
smaller bulblets known as cloves. Use
garlic cloves sparingly to flavour a wide
variety of dishes.

Separate the cloves carefully and plant
just beneath the soil surface, 6–9 in. apart,
during late February. A light, well-
drained, fertile soil open to the sun is
necessary for good results.

HYSSOP

(Hyssopus officinalis. Labiatae)
Mediterranean regions, eastwards to central Asia. Height 18 in. or more; spread
9–12 in. A hardy, sub-shrubby perennial,
with narrow, mid-green, aromatic leaves.
Tubular, two-lipped, blue flowers, $\frac{1}{2}$ in.
long, open from July to September.

HYSSOP

Both leaves and flowers may be used,
fresh or dried, to add their minty flavour
to vegetables, stews and salads.

Hyssop needs a sunny site and well-drained soil. Plant 9–12 in. apart in September and October or March and April. Propagate by 2 in. long cuttings of side-shoots in April or May. Insert in equal parts peat and sand in a cold frame. When rooted, either pot into 3 in. containers of John Innes potting compost No. 1 and plant out in September, or plant direct into the permanent site. Seeds may be sown in April in a well-raked seed bed, progressively thinning the seedlings until the desired spacing is achieved when they are about 3–4 in. tall.

LOVAGE

LOVAGE
(*Ligusticum scoticum. Umbelliferae*)
N.W. Europe. Height up to 24 in.; spread up to 12 in. A perennial plant, with pale to mid-green leaves usually divided into nine toothed, sometimes lobed, ovate leaflets. Erect, sparsely branched stems bear 2–3 in. wide clusters of tiny green-white flowers during July. Flowering stems should be removed when young to promote further young leaves.

The leaves, seeds, stems and roots are used in cooking. The flavour is slightly musky and lemon-like and is well preserved in the dried leaves. The leaves may be used fresh or blanched to flavour soups, and shredded in salads. The stems can be candied and used as a substitute for angelica. The dried seeds can be sprinkled on cakes and biscuits, and the roots can be cooked and served like celeriac.

Lovage requires a well-drained soil open to the sun. Sow the seeds either when ripe in September, or the following March or April, in a well-raked seed bed. Thin or transplant the seedlings 9–12 in. apart, when large enough to handle.

MARJORAM, sweet or knotted
(*Origanum marjorana*, syn. *Marjorana hortensis. Labiatae*)

MARJORAM

Europe. Height up to 24 in., spread 12–18 in. This sub-shrub is not always hardy in Great Britain, and is best grown as a half-hardy annual. It has aromatic, oblong, hairy, somewhat grey-green foliage and tiny tubular white or very pale purple flowers. These are arranged in short clustered spikelets, about $\frac{1}{4}$ in. long, and open from June to September.

The sweetly spiced leaves may be used fresh and are also excellent for drying. The flavour is reminiscent of thyme, and marjoram often replaces this herb in cooking. Its uses include the seasoning of meat, poultry, soups and stews, stuffings and omelettes.

Pot marjoram (*Origanum onites*) is a related species and is fully hardy. It is often cultivated as a substitute for sweet marjoram and has the same uses in the kitchen. The leaves, however, are less sweet, often bitter.

Grow in full sun and in well-drained fertile soil. Sow seeds of sweet marjoram under glass during early March at a temperature of 10–13°C (50–55°F) in pots or pans of John Innes seed compost. Prick out the seedlings, when large enough to handle, into boxes of John Innes potting compost No. 1. Harden off the young plants before planting out in May.

MINT

MINT

(*Mentha spicata, M. rotundifolia. Labiatae*)
Europe, including Great Britain. Height and spread 3 ft or more. The common or spearmint (*M. spicata*) is a vigorous hardy perennial with invasive underground rhizomes. Each square-sectioned stem bears pairs of mid-green, toothed, sword-shaped leaves, with a strong spearmint aroma. From July to September, the upper stems bear numerous 4–6 in. long spikes of pale purple flowers.

Apple mint (*M. rotundifolia*) is of similar growth habit, but is even more robust with larger, white-hairy, broadly ovate to rounded, toothed leaves. The flowers are rose-purple and appear from August to October. This species has a

strong flavour and is particularly recommended for mint sauce.

The leaves are used to flavour young
summer vegetables such as potatoes, peas,
mushrooms and carrots. Sprigs of mint
are refreshing in cool drinks, and the
chopped leaves are used for sauces, jellies
and chutneys.

Grow mint in moisture-retentive soil,
in sun or partial shade. Plant at any time
between October and April. Increase by
division in autumn or spring, cutting the
rhizomes into 4–6 in. lengths and replanting. Alternatively, take 3 in. long cuttings
of young side-shoots in April or May; root
the cuttings in ordinary soil in a cold frame.
When well established, pinch out the
growing points to promote bushy growth.

Fresh mint can be obtained during
winter by lifting rhizomes at four to six-
week intervals from October onwards. Set
in boxes of John Innes potting compost
No. 1 or plant in a bed or border under
glass at a temperature of 13°C (55°F).
The shoots will be ready for use after
about four weeks.

PARSLEY

PARSLEY
(*Petroselinum crispum*, syn. *P. sativum.*
Umbelliferae)
S. Europe, naturalised in Great Britain.
Height 12–24 in.; spread 12 in. A freshly

aromatic perennial herb, usually grown as an annual or biennial. Cultivated varieties, such as 'Giant Curled' and 'Moss Curled', have rich green, intricately cut leaves with curled segments, creating a mossy effect. If allowed to flower, erect branched stems carry 2–3 in. wide flattened heads of tiny green-yellow florets from June to August. Remove the flowering stems when they are small, to promote growth of further young leaves.

Use the leaves fresh in sauces, particularly for fish, in salads, in *bouquets garnis* and, finely chopped, as an ingredient of *fines herbes*. Parsley is the basis of *maître d'hôtel* butter; fresh sprigs are also used for garnishes.

Parsley needs a fertile, well-drained soil, in a sunny or partially shaded site. Sow seeds in February or March for a summer and autumn crop and again in late July for a winter and spring crop. Thin the seedlings to 9 in. apart as soon as they are large enough to handle. In cold areas, protect the plants with cloches from late October onwards.

ROSEMARY

ROSEMARY
(*Rosmarinus officinalis. Labiatae*)
S. Europe, east to Turkey. Height 6–7 ft; spread 5–6 ft. A bushy, hardy evergreen shrub with narrow leaves, mid to deep

green above, almost white beneath; they have a sweet lavender-like fragrance. Pale purple tubular flowers, $\frac{1}{2}-\frac{3}{4}$ in. long and with a broad, three-lobed lower lip, open during April and May. Mature plants may produce a few flowers at almost any time of the year.

Use small sprigs of fresh rosemary to flavour roast lamb and pork, veal, rabbit and grilled fish. The dried leaves may be crumbled and sprinkled over the same meats, but the flavour is more noticeable when used in stuffings. Fresh sprigs can be used in a *bouquet garni*.

Rosemary thrives in any well-drained soil, in a sunny position sheltered from strong north and east winds. If more than one bush is grown, space them 2–3 ft apart. Increase by cuttings of 6 in. long, strong stems planted in permanent sites, in March or September.

Alternatively, especially in exposed areas, take 3 in. long cuttings and insert in equal parts (by volume) peat and sand in a cold frame. Transplant to permanent sites when well rooted.

SAGE

SAGE
(*Salvia officinalis. Labiatae*)
S. Europe. Height and spread up to 24 in. A hardy evergreen shrub with oblong-ovate, wrinkled, grey-green aromatic

leaves. Tubular, blue-purple or white, two-lipped flowers, 1 in. long, are borne in whorled spikes, during June and July.

Fresh or dried leaves are chiefly used in stuffings for pork, chicken and duck. The strong flavour of the fresh leaves is equally suitable for liver and eels.

Grow in any well-drained soil, open to the sun. Plant in March or April and set 15 in. apart. Propagate by 3–4 in. long cuttings taken in August or September. Insert in equal parts (by volume) peat and sand in a cold frame. When rooted, place singly in 3 in. pots of John Innes potting compost No. 1. Plant out the following April. Alternatively, sow seeds in pans of John Innes seed compost in March and place in a cold frame. When the seedlings are large enough to handle, treat as for cuttings and plant out when the pots are full of roots.

SALAD BURNET

SALAD BURNET

(*Sanguisorba minor*, syn. *Poterium sanguisorba. Rosaceae*)
Europe. Height (in flower) 2–3 ft; spread 9–12 in. A tufted hardy perennial, smelling of cucumber when bruised. The leaves are composed of 4–12 pairs of bright mid-green, ovate, toothed leaflets. Branched slender stems carry compact, $\frac{1}{2}$ in. wide, globular heads of tiny green, sometimes

purple-flushed, florets which open from May to September. Removal of the flowering stems encourages the growth of young leaves.

The fresh, finely chopped leaves add flavour to butters and sauces, and they are excellent in salads. The leaves are suitable for freezing.

Grow in light, fertile, well-drained soil, preferably in full sun, although the plants also do well in partial shade. Plant 9–12 in. apart from September to March. Divide in March.

SAVORY, summer
(*Satureja hortensis. Labiatae*)

S. Europe. Height and spread 9–12 in. An erect, sweetly aromatic, hardy annual with narrow, dark-green foliage. Spikes of purple-spotted, white or pale lilac, tubular flowers appear from July to September.

SUMMER SAVORY

The bitter-tasting leaves should be used young, preferably before flowers appear. They impart a minty flavour to salads, and soups, fish and egg dishes, and are particularly good cooked with runner beans. The dried leaves are suitable for stuffings, in sausages and in herb mixtures.

Grow in any well-drained soil, in a sunny position. Sow seeds during April and thin the seedlings to 6–9 in. apart.

SAVORY, winter
(Satureja montana. Labiatae)

S. Europe. This sub-shrubby perennial is similar in appearance to summer savory. It is of slightly more spreading growth, and bears larger flowers.

Cultivate these plants as summer savory, and use the leaves for the same purposes.

Winter savory can also be increased by division in March or April, or by cuttings taken during May. These should be sturdy young shoots, 2 in. long. Insert in equal parts (by volume) peat and sand in a cold frame. Set the rooted cuttings in 3 in. pots of John Innes potting compost No. 1 and plant out the following April.

SORREL, French
(Rumex scutatus. Polygonaceae)

SORREL

W. Asia, N. Africa, Europe, naturalised in Great Britain. Height and spread 12–18 in. This tufted hardy perennial has slightly fleshy, triangular, smooth, grey-green leaves. Tiny, green-yellow, red-tinted flowers are borne in narrow loose clusters, 6–8 in. long, from June to September. Remove the flowers to encourage the production of leaves.

The bitter young leaves are used raw in salads; they may also be treated like spinach and made into a purée with butter, to be served with veal, pork, fish and eggs. Blanched, finely chopped leaves are used to flavour soups.

French sorrel needs a moisture-retentive soil, preferably in a sunny position. Plant at any time from September to March, setting the plants about 9–12 in. apart. Increase by division in March. Alternatively, sow seeds in March or April, thinning the seedlings to the desired spacing when large enough.

TARRAGON
(*Artemisia dracunculus. Compositae*)
W. and S. Europe, Asia, U.S.A. Height and spread 18 in. or more. An aromatic perennial, fully hardy in sheltered positions in well-drained soil. The lower dark grey-green leaves are lance-shaped and toothed; the upper leaves are entire. Nodding green-white flowers are borne in loose clusters in August.

TARRAGON

Pick the leaves young, preferably before the flowers appear; they are suitable for freezing. The chopped leaves are essential to *fines herbes* mixtures, and are used in sauces, butters and in creamed soups. Tarragon leaves are used in vinegars for salads and mayonnaise.

Grow in fertile, well-drained soil, in full sun. Plant in October or March. Increase tarragon by division and replanting of the roots in April.

37

THYME, common
(*Thymus vulgaris. Labiatae*)

S. Europe, Spain to Italy. Height 4–8 in.; spread 12 in. This herb forms a spreading wiry-stemmed shrublet clad with narrowly oblong, aromatic, mid to deep green leaves. Tiny, tubular, lilac flowers appear in crowded heads, 1 in. long, in June and continue until August.

Common thyme, as well as the related lemon thyme, is a pungent herb, and an essential part of a *bouquet garni*. Use the leaves, fresh or dried, to flavour soups, vegetables, fish, savoury meat dishes and stuffings for poultry.

This plant requires a well-drained soil and a sunny site. Plant 9–12 in. apart, at any time from September to April. Propagate by taking 2 in. long cuttings and inserting them in equal parts (by volume) peat and sand in a cold frame during May or June. Set the cuttings singly in 3 in. pots of John Innes potting compost No. 1 when rooted, and plant out in September.

The plants may also be divided and replanted in March or April. Alternatively, sow seeds in spring in pans of John Innes seed compost and place in a cold frame. When the seedlings are large enough to handle, pot up in 3 in. pots of John Innes potting compost No. 1. Set out in permanent sites in September.

THYME

The use of herbs

THERE are no strict rules governing the use of herbs in cooking. Certain herbs have become associated with particular foods—for instance, mint with lamb, parsley or mint with vegetables, and sage with duck—but these are often national or even regional preferences. The use of flavouring is entirely a matter of taste, and any herb or combination of herbs may be used. With a constant supply of fresh, frozen or dried herbs readily available, the choice of combinations and experiments is large.

The lists which follow are merely guides to the use of herbs. The creative cook must experiment to determine which herbs have the most pleasing flavour and in what proportions they should be used. However, herbs should always be used with discretion as their purpose is to enhance and complement the flavour of a dish, not to mask it. Take special care with dried herbs which often have more flavouring effect than fresh or frozen leaves.

Unless otherwise stated, a *bouquet garni* consists of a sprig of parsley, a sprig of thyme and a bay leaf, tied together or wrapped in a piece of muslin so that they can easily be removed from the cooked dish. Occasionally, additional herbs or pieces of vegetable may be included for extra flavour.

SOUPS

GENERAL. Fresh herbs make excellent garnishes. Finely chopped parsley or chervil is suitable for most soups. With strong meaty soups, try chopped chives or celery leaves; chopped dill or fennel leaves are good with fish soups.

MIXED VEGETABLE. Any one or two of the following herbs may be included in a *bouquet garni*: celery, dill, rosemary, marjoram, basil, sage, tarragon. Savory, hyssop and fennel are useful in small quantities. Italian minestrone soup varies from region to region and includes the following herbs: combinations of basil, sage and celery leaves (Milan); parsley, marjoram and rosemary (Trento); basil and rosemary, or basil and borage (Genoa); and basil, celery leaves, rosemary and thyme (Tuscany).

CONSOMMÉ. Add to the *bouquet garni* a sprig of tarragon and finely shredded aromatic root vegetables, such as carrot or parsnip.

BEEF. Include basil or marjoram in the *bouquet garni*.

MUTTON. Mint, rosemary or dill are recommended as additions to the *bouquet garni*.

CHICKEN. Add tarragon, marjoram, sage and rosemary; or sage to the *bouquet garni*.

PEA. Include mint in the *bouquet garni*.

CARROT. Dill and anise add distinctive flavours.

TOMATO. A sprig of basil, mint or marjoram may be added to the *bouquet garni*.

FISH

Parsley, chervil and celery are ideal with mild-flavoured types of fish and shellfish. Stronger and more oily fish will take the more insistent flavours of dill, bay, fennel, basil, tarragon, marjoram, thyme, sage, balm and rosemary, either singly or in combinations of two or three. Garlic may be used sparingly with mussels. Grilled fish may be seasoned with mint, sage or rosemary.

MEAT

BEEF. Tarragon and parsley both go well with steak, especially in herb butters. In casseroles and stews, the French traditionally use a *bouquet garni*; in Italy, rosemary, basil, marjoram and sage are popular. Ground coriander, much used in the East, is excellent in a steak and kidney pudding. Caraway seed is a traditional and distinctive ingredient of a goulash.

LAMB OR MUTTON. Fresh mint sauce is the usual English accompaniment to roast lamb. Lamb can be roasted with rosemary and garlic, or with combinations of basil, origano and sweet marjoram. Other herbs for roasts and stews are dill, fennel, coriander or caraway seeds and juniper berries.

PORK. The richness of the meat requires strong flavourings, such as sage, thyme, rosemary, bay or marjoram, singly or in combinations. Caraway seeds with garlic are used in Austria, fennel seeds, juniper berries or sometimes anise in Sardinia.

VEAL. The delicate flavour is easily masked. Parsley may be used freely; sage, thyme, marjoram, bay and tarragon are also good, but should be added sparingly.

LIVER. In Mediterranean countries, rosemary, bay, parsley, sage and celery leaves are popular flavourings. Liver cooked in wine with garlic, with or without other herbs, is excellent.

KIDNEYS. These are usually cooked with parsley.

POULTRY AND GAME

CHICKEN. Almost any combination of herbs may be used. Garlic and a *bouquet garni* may be improved by the addition of tarragon and parsley; parsley and marjoram; parsley, celery leaves and basil; sage and fennel; or dill, lemon thyme, tarragon and celery.

DUCK. Parsley, thyme and celery leaves go well together. Rosemary, basil, sage, marjoram or a mixture of these may be used, often combined with garlic.

GOOSE. The rich flesh needs strong flavouring. Sage is often used; also recommended are combinations of rosemary, bay and garlic; or bay, lemon thyme, basil and tarragon.

PARTRIDGE. The strong and distinctive flavour is complemented by thyme, marjoram or rosemary, or by a *bouquet garni*. Roast partridge is excellent with a salad of fresh tarragon, chervil and chives.

PHEASANT. Celery gives a pleasant flavour, together with the usual *bouquet garni*.

VENISON. This strongly flavoured meat may be tough, and is best marinated before cooking, in wine or wine and vinegar. The marinade may be seasoned with a *bouquet garni* containing a few juniper berries; or with sage, rosemary and celery leaves.

VEGETABLES AND SALADS

BEANS. Cook with a sprig of parsley or savory.

BEETROOT. Chopped chives, tarragon or parsley go well with beetroot salad.

CARROTS. Use fresh parsley and lemon juice in salads, or cook with parsley, anise or garlic.

PEAS. Cook or garnish with parsley or mint.

POTATOES. Chopped parsley, dill, chives or mint are excellent in salads. A bay leaf improves the taste of boiled potatoes. Rosemary, dill or green coriander give an unusual flavour to casserole potatoes.

TOMATOES. Basil or marjoram enhance the flavour of both cooked and raw tomatoes. Parsley, mint or chopped chives are also suitable in tomato salads.

GREEN SALADS. A sprinkling of *fines herbes* (a mixture of finely chopped parsley, tarragon, chives and chervil) is excellent on any salad. Dill, fennel, anise or sorrel are particularly good with grated cabbage.

SAUCES AND BUTTERS

Most green herbs can be used to make herb butters; parsley, tarragon, shallots and chervil are the most usual flavourings. Parsley, dill, fennel, mint, celery leaves and chervil are used to flavour sauces.

OMELETTES

The classic *omelette aux fines herbes* contains a mixture of finely chopped parsley, tarragon, chervil and chives. Most green herbs are also good on their own, particularly parsley, mint, salad burnet and lovage.

SWEETS AND CAKES

A bay leaf gives a pleasant flavour to baked rice pudding. Fresh mint makes an attractive and fragrant garnish for fresh fruit salads and sweets. Fresh young leaves of sweet basil, mint and other soft-leaved herbs can be pounded with sugar to make herb sugars, useful for flavouring cakes. Caraway seeds are used in cakes and breads.

DRINKS

Herb teas—infusions of fresh or dried leaves of chamomile, dill, parsley or lime—are popular in Europe. Mint leaves may be added to either hot or iced tea; borage, mint and balm are good in fruit drinks and cups.

VINEGARS

Wine vinegar may be flavoured with dill, tarragon, thyme, chervil, basil, marjoram or mixed herbs. Herb vinegars are excellent for pickling and for giving extra seasoning to salad dressings and mayonnaise.

Recipes

Herbs give the best flavour when fresh but, except when used as garnishes, frozen or dried leaves can usually be substituted. Dried herbs should generally be used in half the quantity recommended for fresh herbs, but the amount can be varied according to taste.

The following recipes serve four to six people.

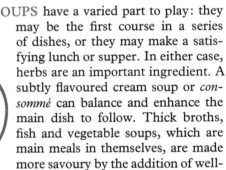

Soups have a varied part to play: they may be the first course in a series of dishes, or they may make a satisfying lunch or supper. In either case, herbs are an important ingredient. A subtly flavoured cream soup or *consommé* can balance and enhance the main dish to follow. Thick broths, fish and vegetable soups, which are main meals in themselves, are made more savoury by the addition of well-chosen herbs. A *bouquet garni* is one of the secrets of a well-flavoured stock. A sprig of basil, added to the stock, improves the flavour of fish and vegetable soups.

ROMANIAN CIORBA

(Sour soup with meat balls)

This refreshing summer soup is cooked by peasants in the plains of Romania. The traditional souring agent is verjuice—the boiled juice of unripe plums or grapes. Lemon juice makes a suitable substitute.

2 pints beef stock	1 egg
1 large onion	1 slice stale bread
3 carrots	milk
3 sticks celery	dill leaves
1 sprig thyme or	salt and pepper
marjoram	lemon juice
½ lb. minced beef	lovage leaves

Chop the vegetables finely and set aside about one-third of the onion. Add the remainder with the carrot and celery to the stock and simmer until tender, together with the thyme; pepper and salt to taste.

Meanwhile, cut the bread into cubes and soak them in a little milk. Add these, with salt, pepper, chopped dill and the remainder of the onion, to the minced beef and mix well, binding the mixture with a beaten egg. Form teaspoonfuls of the mixture into balls, using floured hands, and poach for 15 minutes in the soup, after having removed the sprig of thyme.

Before serving, add sufficient lemon juice to make the soup pleasantly sour, season to taste, and sprinkle in a good handful of chopped lovage.

NORWEGIAN CARAWAY SOUP

The fresh young leaves of the caraway plant have a mild, almost parsley-like flavour, quite different from the pungent taste of the seeds. In Norway, this soup is traditionally made in spring, when the green shoots appear. It is sufficiently sustaining to make a supper dish.

2 pints veal or
   chicken stock
1 oz. butter
1 oz. flour
1 cup finely chopped
   caraway leaves

1 cup coarsely chopped
   caraway leaves
1 egg yolk
2 tablespoons cream
salt and pepper
poached eggs

Melt the butter and stir in the flour. Cook gently for 1 minute, then add the finely chopped caraway leaves. Add the stock, a little at a time, keeping the pan on a low heat and stirring continuously to prevent lumps. When all the stock has been incorporated, simmer the soup for a further 5 minutes.

Beat together the cream and egg yolk. Add the coarsely chopped caraway leaves to the soup and remove from the heat. Pour a little of the soup into the egg and cream, blend well and mix in with the soup in the pan. Stir the soup gently and reheat over a low fire for a few minutes. Do not allow the soup to boil.

Serve in individual soup bowls, floating a poached egg in each bowl. Hot buttered toast can accompany this lunch or supper dish.

L'AIGO BOULIDO
(French sage soup)

Like French onion soup, this traditional Provençal soup is credited with restorative powers and is said to ward off colds. It is extremely easy and economical to prepare, and requires little cooking time.

2 pints water	*1 sprig sage*
salt and pepper	*1 sprig thyme*
7–8 cloves garlic	*1 bay leaf*
4 slices bread	*2 egg yolks*
olive oil	

Boil the water and add salt and pepper to taste. Crush six of the garlic cloves with the blade of a knife and add to the water. Simmer for 5 minutes. Rub the remaining garlic lightly over the slices of bread (white or brown), sprinkle them with a few drops of olive oil, and place one slice in each soup bowl or plate.

Remove the water from the heat and throw in the sage, thyme and bay leaf. Allow to brew, like tea, for 3 minutes. Strain through a fine sieve into another pan.

Beat the egg yolks lightly and stir in a little of the liquid; mix well and stir into the remaining liquid to thicken it. Add salt and pepper and reheat if necessary, but do not allow to boil. Pour the soup over the bread in each of the bowls.

A richer soup can be made by using mayonnaise instead of eggs to bind the liquid.

FISH of all types, including shellfish, is greatly improved by additional flavours. Many of the classic fish dishes depend on the use of herbs, usually in the accompanying sauces. Plain grilled fish can be improved by a sprinkling of herbs before cooking. Alternatively, the fish may be stuffed with herbs pounded with lemon juice and chopped onion or garlic, then grilled or fried. Herb butters may be served with fish as an alternative to a complicated sauce. Fish, steeped before cooking in a marinade of white wine and herbs, absorbs a subtle flavour; the marinade then forms the basis of the accompanying sauce. Fish should never be boiled, but steamed or gently poached in a stock flavoured with parsley, bay leaves and sage.

BASS FLAMBÉ ON FENNEL

This is a well-known dish from Southern France. Mackerel or trout may be substituted for bass. The fish is flamed on the feathery leaves of fennel.

Wash and dry a large bunch of fennel leaves and place in the bottom of a grill pan, setting the grid over them. Clean and split the fish and score it with a knife; place on the grid, brush with oil or butter and season with salt and pepper. Grill, turning once or twice.

When the fish is cooked, warm a tot of brandy in a

49

ladle, set it alight and pour over the fish and fennel, allowing the fennel to catch fire. Serve immediately the flames have died down. The fish will be impregnated with the flavours of brandy and fennel.

Barbecued mackerel or trout, served on a bed of fresh fennel leaves, makes an excellent picnic dish.

MACKEREL WITH FENNEL SAUCE
Like the previous recipe, this English dish makes use of the feathery leaves of fennel.

6 mackerel	1 oz. flour
1½ oz. butter	approx. ¾ pint water
1 heaped tablespoon chopped fennel	salt and pepper

Melt 1 oz. butter and add the fennel; cook for a few seconds, then blend in the flour. Add the water a little at a time, beating smooth between each addition. When the sauce reaches the desired consistency, cook for a few minutes more, then add salt and pepper to taste. Remove from the heat. Dot the surface with knobs of butter and stand the pan in a larger pan of hot water to keep warm while the mackerel are being grilled.

Pour the sauce over the mackerel and serve.

EELS IN DILL SAUCE
This recipe comes from Germany, where eels are a popular fish. Eels should always be absolutely fresh for cooking.

The recipe is also suitable for other oily fish, such as herring and mackerel.

1 eel	*3 peppercorns*
1 cup vinegar	*pinch of sage*
1 cup white wine	*1 teaspoon cornflour*
2 cups water	*milk*
1 onion	*4 tablespoons sour*
1 leek	*cream*
2–3 carrots	*2 egg yolks*
bunch parsley stalks	*salt and pepper*
2 bay leaves	*2 tablespoons chopped*
3 cloves	*dill*

Make a stock from the diced vegetables, parsley stalks, bay leaves, peppercorns, cloves and sage simmered for 15 minutes in the vinegar, wine and water. Add salt to make the liquid fairly salty.

Meanwhile, clean and skin the eel and cut into 4-in. pieces; wash them thoroughly in cold water to remove all blood. Poach the eel in the stock for about 20 minutes, and leave in the liquid.

Pour off 1 cupful of the stock into another pan, and heat; thicken with the cornflour mixed with milk, and boil for a moment or two, then remove from the heat. Beat in the cream and the egg yolks, add the chopped dill and season. Add the pieces of eel and turn them carefully to coat them with the sauce.

Serve with boiled potatoes and cucumber salad.

EATS benefit from the subtle use of herbs. Delicately flavoured meat, such as veal, is easily overpowered by the stronger herbs and these must be used sparingly. Strong-flavoured herbs may be used liberally on a full-flavoured meat such as pork. Like fish, meat may be sprinkled with herbs before grilling or roasting, and herb butters make excellent garnishes. Meats for braising or stewing are improved by first marinating them in wine with herbs.

LAMB WITH GARLIC AND ROSEMARY

The combination of rosemary and garlic with lamb is typical of Mediterranean countries; it gives a strong flavour to the meat. This dish can also be made with savory, but this bitter herb is more powerful than rosemary and should be used sparingly.

leg or shoulder of lamb
3–6 cloves garlic
3–6 sprigs rosemary
salt
black pepper
oil or melted
* butter*
1 glass white wine

Make several deep incisions in the joint with a sharp knife, right down to the bone. Press a clove of garlic and a sprig of rosemary into each incision. Rub the skin with salt and pepper and brush with oil or melted butter. Wrap the meat in foil and cook in a moderate oven for 1 hour; remove the foil and continue to cook until thoroughly done. Pour the wine over the meat about 15 minutes before the end of the cooking time.

Serve with the gravy made of the wine and meat juices. Roasted parsnips and sweet potatoes go well with it.

BAKED PORK CHOPS
Juniper is much used in mountainous regions of Europe where it grows wild. It combines well with other herbs.

4 large pork chops	*1 glass red wine*
chopped fennel	*1 cup veal stock*
a few juniper berries	*salt and pepper*
1 lemon	*¼ lb. mushrooms*
olive oil	*butter*

Rub the chops with salt and pepper, scatter chopped fennel and crushed juniper berries over each; sprinkle with juice of half the lemon, and olive oil. Place the chops in a baking dish and allow to stand for at least 2 hours, so that the flavours are absorbed. Then add the wine and stock, and the remainder of the lemon juice. Cover, and simmer in a moderate oven for $1-1\frac{1}{2}$ hours.

Ten minutes before serving, thicken the gravy with cornflour, and add the mushrooms which have been lightly cooked in butter.

BEEF IN RED WINE

This rich, highly flavoured stew may also be cooked as a casserole in a slow oven. The rump steak may then be replaced by less expensive stewing steak.

2 lb. rump steak	2 bay leaves
2 glasses red wine	2 bacon rashers
2 onions	1 cup beef stock
2–3 cloves garlic	1 teaspoon each, chopped
1 sprig parsley	parsley, marjoram
1 sprig marjoram	and basil
1 sprig basil	salt and pepper

Prepare a marinade of the wine, 1 sliced onion, the crushed cloves of garlic and the sprigs of herbs. Cube or slice the meat, sprinkle it with pepper, and put it in the marinade to steep for a few hours, turning occasionally. Remove the meat and strain the marinade.

Chop the second onion and the rashers of bacon; fry these in a large pan until the bacon is crisp and the onions slightly browned. Remove from the pan and add the meat. Brown this thoroughly in the bacon fat, then return the bacon and onion, and pour in the marinade. Allow to bubble for a few minutes, then add the beef stock and the freshly chopped herbs.

Cover the pan and simmer gently for 1½–2 hours, or until the meat is tender and the gravy has reduced. Adjust the seasoning before serving. Buttered carrots and baked or boiled potatoes make good accompaniments.

PASTEL DE CHOCLO

(Chilean corn pie)

With slight variations, this unusual dish is popular in most South American countries. Essentially, it is an aromatic shepherd's pie, with a topping of corn instead of potato. Fresh corn is best, but tinned corn may be used.

1 lb. minced beef	*6 cobs of corn, or 2 tins*
1 onion	*of grain corn*
olive oil	*½ cup milk*
¼ cup seeded raisins	*pinch of cinnamon*
pinch of cumin	*1 teaspoon chopped basil*
10 black olives	*2 tablespoons butter*
salt and pepper	*2 beaten eggs*
2 hard-boiled eggs	*granulated sugar*

Chop the onion finely and fry it gently in the oil until just transparent. Remove from the pan and fry the mince until lightly browned. Add the onion, raisins, cumin, a dash of pepper and a little salt. Continue cooking, adding water if necessary, until the meat is tender. Add the olives, but remember that these are salty. Place the mixture in a baking dish in layers with alternate layers of hard-boiled egg.

Grate the corn from the cobs, or pound the canned grains to a pulp, and place in a saucepan. Add the milk, butter, cinnamon, basil and a pinch of salt. Stir over a medium heat until the corn is cooked and the mixture is of a thick dropping consistency. Remove from the heat and stir in the beaten eggs. Pour over the top of the meat and sprinkle liberally with granulated sugar.

Bake in a hot oven until the sugar browns.

COARSE COUNTRY FARE

This rough-textured, meaty *terrine* is suitable as an appetiser. It may also constitute the main course, served with a green salad and fresh, crusty bread.

1 lb. belly of pork, or	*1 teaspoon each, chopped*
other cheap cut	*fennel, lemon thyme*
1 lb. lean veal	*and parsley*
½ lb. cooked ham	*1 glass white wine*
4 oz. breadcrumbs	*1 tot sherry or brandy*
2–3 cloves garlic	*2 bay leaves*
pepper and salt	*6 bacon rashers*

Mince the veal and pork together and mix in the finely chopped cooked ham. Add the breadcrumbs, crushed garlic cloves, chopped herbs and a little salt, bearing in mind that the ham is salty. Pour the wine and sherry over the mixture and leave to soak for 2–3 hours.

Place three rashers of bacon and a bay leaf in the bottom of a *terrine* dish; add the meat mixture, pressing it down firmly. Lay the other bacon rashers and bay leaf on top. Stand the dish in a baking tray half full of water, and cook in a moderate oven for 2½ hours. When the *terrine* has cooled, cover with paper and place a weight on top for a few hours before turning out.

POULTRY AND GAME includes meats of very different flavours and strengths. The mildness of chicken is complemented by almost any herb, but duck, goose, hare and rabbit all have stronger and more distinctive flavours and need the more pungent herbs. Game birds and venison, which are hung, are the strongest meats of all and will take liberal amounts of herbs. The following recipes include casseroles, a marinade and a stuffing, and an excellent *pâté*.

POULET À L'ESTRAGON
(Chicken with tarragon)
Originally a classic French recipe, this title is now given to several different dishes, having in common only the basic combination of chicken and tarragon.

1 chicken	*1 sprig tarragon*
1 tablespoon butter	*salt and pepper*
1¼ cups white wine	*tarragon butter*

Joint the chicken into serving pieces and brown them in the butter, using a large, deep frying pan. Add the wine, tarragon, salt and pepper. Cover and cook gently for about 30 minutes, or until the chicken is tender. Serve garnished with pats of tarragon butter.

CHICKEN WITH PARSLEY AND GARLIC

The parsley in this recipe must be fresh, since it forms the bulk of the richly flavoured wine sauce.

1 chicken	*1 sprig thyme*
1 tablespoon oil	*1 glass white wine*
1 tablespoon butter	*salt*
1 onion	*black pepper*
2–3 cloves garlic	*1 large bunch parsley*
1 bay leaf	*1 lemon*

Joint the chicken and brown lightly in the oil and butter in a large frying pan. Remove from the pan and add the onion and 1 or 2 cloves of garlic, all finely chopped. Cook until glazed, add a bay leaf and sprig of thyme, and return the chicken. Pour in the wine, add pepper and salt and cover the pan. Simmer for 30 minutes.

Meanwhile, chop very finely the parsley, a clove of garlic and a piece of lemon peel; if possible pound them together in a mortar.

When the chicken is cooked, remove the thyme and bay leaf and add the chopped parsley mixture. If necessary, moisten with a little more wine. Cook just long enough to soften the parsley and incorporate it into the sauce. Adjust the seasoning. Serve, garnished with lemon slices.

GLAZED DUCK

Attractively garnished and served with a salad, this is an excellent dish for a cold buffet or party spread.

1 duck	*1 teaspoon each, chopped*
3–4 rashers streaky bacon	*parsley, thyme*
1 onion	*and basil*
2 cloves garlic	*1 glass white wine*
pinch of mace	*1 orange*

Chop the onion and garlic finely and pound together with the herbs and mace. Spread the mixture over the bacon rashers and place these over the breast and sides of the bird. Place in a casserole dish, pour on the wine, and cover. Cook in a slow oven for 3–4 hours.

Remove the bird from the oven and allow to cool. Lift off the solidified fat from the surface of the gravy and discard. Pour off the gravy into a small pan and warm until runny. Pour over the duck, spooning up the excess and returning it to the pan. As each layer of coating sets, follow it with another application, until all the liquid has been used. Garnish with slices of orange.

CONIGLIO ARROSTO
(Rabbit with herbs and black olives)
This traditional hunters' dish from the Italian Riviera makes use of the local small black olives and wild herbs.

1 rabbit	*1 bay leaf*
olive oil	*1 sprig thyme*
1 onion	*1 sprig rosemary*
2–3 cloves garlic	*1 cup white wine*
1 large tomato	*a handful black olives*

Cut up the rabbit into serving pieces, wash and dry thoroughly. Heat the oil in a large, deep frying pan and fry the rabbit over a high heat until deeply browned.

Peel the tomato, squeeze out and discard the seeds, and chop the flesh coarsely. Add this, with the chopped onion and garlic, to the rabbit, and continue to fry until the vegetable mixture is browned. Reduce the heat and add the herbs. When the juices begin to dry, pour in the wine and cover the pan. Simmer for about 1 hour, or until the meat is tender, turning the pieces once or twice. About 15–20 minutes before serving, put in the olives.

MARINADE FOR VENISON

Venison is a tough meat, and should be marinated. A marinade adds flavour, breaks down the fibres and tenderises the meat. This recipe is also suitable for beef.

1 onion	*1 teaspoon each, chopped*
1 stick celery	*thyme and marjoram*
1 carrot	*3–4 black peppercorns*
olive oil	*1 teaspoon ground coriander*
2–3 cloves garlic	*½ bottle red wine*
1 bay leaf	

Brown the sliced onion, chopped celery and chopped carrot in the oil. After a few minutes, add the other ingredients and simmer for about 15 minutes. Allow the marinade to cool and then pour over the venison. Allow to soak for two days if possible, before cooking.

CHICKEN AND CHESTNUT PÂTÉ

This *pâté* tastes best if the flavour is allowed to blend and develop for two days after cooking. Serve cold, accompanied by hot buttered toast.

1 tablespoon butter	*2 oz. fresh breadcrumbs*
1 small onion	*1 teaspoon each, chopped*
2–3 cloves garlic	*parsley, chives and*
4 bacon rashers	*lemon thyme*
6 oz. chicken livers	*salt and pepper*
6 oz. lean pork or veal	*1 egg*
4 oz. cooked chicken	*1 tot brandy or sherry*
1 large tin unsweetened	*1 bay leaf*
chestnut purée	

Fry the onion, garlic and two rashers of bacon, all finely chopped, until the onion is transparent. Add the chopped chicken livers and continue to cook gently for 5 minutes.

Meanwhile, mince together the pork and cooked chicken and mix these with the chestnut purée, breadcrumbs, salt, pepper and herbs (omitting the bay leaf). Bind the mixture with the lightly beaten egg and add the brandy.

Add the cooked ingredients; for a *pâté* of finer texture, grind them down or liquidise them first. Press the *pâté* firmly into a buttered *terrine* dish and place the bay leaf and the remaining bacon, cut into strips, on top. Set the dish in a baking tray half full of water, and bake in a moderate oven for $1\frac{1}{2}$–2 hours. When cool, cover with paper and place a weight on top for a few hours.

EGETABLES AND SALADS can be made more interesting by the addition of well-chosen herbs. A sprinkling of chopped parsley or chives over boiled vegetables, and mint leaves cooked with fresh garden peas, are well-known herb choices, but many of the less-common herbs are equally good. Suitably chosen herbs can turn an ordinary vegetable into a dish for a dinner party. Almost any vegetable can be made into an unusual salad with a herb-flavoured dressing.

ROSEMARY POTATO PIE

Most herbs go well with potatoes, especially when cooked slowly in the oven with milk and butter. The following recipe uses rosemary and onion and is particularly good served with ham or any dry meat which has no sauce.

2 lb. potatoes	salt and pepper
1 lb. onions	rosemary sprigs
1 oz. flour	2–3 oz. butter
$\frac{1}{4}$–$\frac{1}{2}$ pint milk	

Butter a baking dish. Slice the potatoes and onions thinly and fill the dish with alternate layers, sprinkling each layer with milk, flour, salt, freshly ground black pepper and finely chopped rosemary tips, then dot with butter.

Finish with a layer of potato. When completed, the milk should come about halfway up the dish.

Cover the dish and cook in a moderate oven for about $1\frac{1}{2}$ hours, until the liquid is absorbed and the potatoes are soft and impregnated with the rosemary.

BEETROOT IN SOUR CREAM

Beetroot is often a neglected vegetable, usually served cold in a marinade of vinegar and oil, or as a pickle, with cold meats and salads. It does, however, make an excellent hot vegetable and is used as such in Northern and Eastern Europe. The following recipe comes from Russia.

1 lb. beetroot	*$\frac{1}{2}$ bouillon cube*
1 onion	*sugar, salt, pepper and*
1 tablespoon butter	*lemon juice*
$\frac{1}{2}$ pint sour cream	*handful of dill*

Twist the leaves off the beet and wash the beet gently. Boil until tender, in water with a few drops of vinegar. When cooked, remove the tops and roots, and slide off the skins. Chop coarsely.

Chop the onion finely and cook in butter until just transparent. Add the sour cream and crumble in the bouillon cube. Add sugar, lemon juice and salt and pepper to taste. Chop the dill leaves finely and add most of them to the sauce.

Serve with the hot sauce poured over the chopped beet, with the remainder of the chopped dill sprinkled on top.

STUFFED COURGETTES

The spicy flavour of costmary is combined with parsley in this recipe from Turin, Northern Italy.

4 courgettes
½ lb. lean veal
2 oz. pork sausage meat
a little butter
handful of parsley
1 leaf costmary
1 clove garlic

2 eggs
2 heaped tablespoons grated parmesan cheese
grated nutmeg
salt and pepper
white wine

Cook the diced veal and the sausage meat in a little butter. Add the chopped parsley, costmary and garlic, and put the whole mixture through a mincer. Add the parmesan cheese and 2 beaten eggs. Season with grated nutmeg, salt and pepper. Divide the mixture into 8 portions.

Cut the courgettes in half lengthways and scoop out most of the flesh. Fill with the stuffing, and lay them in a buttered baking dish. Dot with butter and sprinkle on a little white wine. Bake for 1 hour in a medium oven, or until tender, basting occasionally with white wine.

POTATO SALAD

The potatoes used for this must be firm, of a waxy texture. Cook them in their skins and pull off the skins as soon as they can be handled. Slice or cube the potatoes while still warm. To each pound of potatoes, add a heaped table-spoon of chopped chives and a warmed dressing made of 4 tablespoons chicken stock or water, 1 tablespoon vinegar, 3 tablespoons oil, and salt to taste. Mix lightly and leave for several hours to cool. Serve with a generous sprinkling of chopped herbs: parsley, chervil, celery leaves, dill or lovage.

CUCUMBER MINT SALAD
Stir together 1 pint yogurt, 1 crushed garlic clove and ½ teaspoon sea salt. Add 1 cup of coarsely grated cucumber and 1 teaspoon finely chopped mint. Mix well and chill for 30 minutes to allow the flavours to blend.

CUCUMBER SALAD
Wash, but do not skin the cucumber. Slice it finely and sprinkle with salt. Leave for 15–30 minutes, then put the slices in a clean cloth and squeeze out all the moisture. Put in a serving dish and sprinkle on freshly ground black pepper and a mixture of 2 parts oil to 1 part wine vinegar. Cover with sour cream (or yogurt) and a generous scattering of chopped dill or chives. Mix and serve chilled with spring chicken or roast veal.

TOMATO SALAD
This salad should be prepared just before serving. Choose large firm tomatoes and slice them evenly. Arrange the slices overlapping on the serving dish. Sprinkle with sea salt, freshly ground black pepper, shredded basil leaves, and finally with a small quantity of olive oil.

SAUCES AND BUTTERS are used to garnish and improve the flavour of all types of food, and here herbs play an important role. Many of the classic sauces are well known, but other excellent sauces can be made by adding different herbs to a basic white or wine sauce, or mayonnaise. Herb butters are made by pounding fresh chopped herbs with a little coarse salt and then blending in butter, a little at a time. The butter fat absorbs and traps the aromatic essential oils which would otherwise soon be lost. Herb butter can be made in a liquidiser, but a mortar and pestle gives the best results. Herb butters will keep in a refrigerator for a few days.

HOT GREEN SAUCE

This is a variable sauce; the herbs used depend on the type of meat, fish or vegetable which the sauce will accompany. A combination of parsley, chervil, sorrel, cress and tarragon is good with most foods.

Make a basic sauce: gently cook 1 oz. flour in 1 oz. butter for a minute or two, then add milk, white wine or stock, little by little, stirring all the time. The sauce should have the consistency of thick cream. Simmer very gently for 10 minutes.

Chop the herbs finely, with added shallot and garlic if

desired; pound with coarse salt, preferably using a mortar and pestle. Tarragon should first be softened in boiling water and then pounded separately, to make sure it disintegrates completely.

Stir the pulverised herbs into the sauce, with salt and pepper to taste. Place a knob of butter on the surface, and keep the sauce hot, in a double saucepan.

Stir in the butter just before serving.

MAÎTRE D'HÔTEL BUTTER
Pound a handful of chopped parsley in a mortar with a little coarse salt. Blend in enough butter to absorb all the parsley. Add a few drops of lemon juice to taste. Serve with grilled steak and fish.

MAYONNAISE
Many cooks fight shy of making their own mayonnaise, but it is fairly simple if these points are remembered:

The eggs should be neither very fresh nor stale, and must be at room temperature. Add a little lemon juice or vinegar to the yolks before the oil. To prevent the mixture from separating, add only a few drops of oil at a time and beat thoroughly before adding more oil.

2 egg yolks	*1 cup olive oil*
2 tablespoons lemon juice	*salt and pepper*
or mild vinegar	

Beat the egg yolks until thick and creamy and beat in

$\frac{1}{2}$ teaspoon lemon juice. Add a dribble of oil and beat until thick. Continue to add the oil, a few drops at a time, beating until fully absorbed between each addition. When the oil has been used up, beat in the remaining lemon juice and season to taste.

MINT SAUCE

Finely chop a handful of fresh apple mint leaves. Boil together $\frac{1}{2}$ cup of white malt or wine vinegar and $\frac{1}{4}$ cup of granulated sugar. When the sugar has dissolved, pour over the chopped mint and leave until cold.

GARLIC BUTTER

This is the butter usually served with snails, but it is equally good with anything from mussels to baked potatoes and hot bread.

$\frac{1}{2}$ lb. butter	*$1\frac{1}{2}$ oz. garlic cloves*
1 oz. parsley	*1 small shallot*

Chop the shallot and garlic and pound them, with a pinch of coarse salt, to a paste. Add the chopped parsley and continue pounding. Add the butter a little at a time, beating well between each addition, until the mixture resembles a fine green ointment. Adjust the seasoning.

SAUCE TARTARE

Add finely chopped parsley, chives, tarragon and capers to a mayonnaise. Serve with grilled or fried fish.

ICKLES AND VINEGARS are often improved by herbs. Indeed, some pickles rely on certain herbs for their distinctive taste. Coriander is a feature of many Indian chutneys, and the sharp flavour of dill is used in pickling gherkins. Herb vinegars are easily made: fill a screw-top jar two-thirds full with leafy tips of the chosen herb and pour on warm vinegar. Cover the mouth of the jar with foil or waxed paper before screwing on the lid. Allow to steep for about two weeks, shaking the jar at least once a day. The vinegar may be strained off or left with the leaves.

GREEN CORIANDER CHUTNEY

This fresh-tasting chutney is easily made and is a good accompaniment to curries, roast meats, toasted cheese and egg dishes. Use fresh coconut for the best flavour.

½ coconut
or ¼ lb. desiccated coconut
a generous handful fresh
  coriander leaves

2–3 hot green chillies
salt
lemon juice

Break the coconut into pieces, cut out the white flesh, and grate it as finely as possible. Desiccated coconut should be softened in a little hot water. Cut open the chillies and carefully remove all the seeds, then chop the flesh and the coriander leaves. Pound the two together in a mortar or basin.

When the mixture is a smooth paste, add the coconut, a little at a time, pounding thoroughly. Finally, add salt and lemon juice to taste. Chopped raw onion may also be included; it should be pounded down with the chillies and coriander leaves before adding the coconut. This chutney is an excellent side-dish to serve with curry and rice, and with roast meat, cheese and egg dishes.

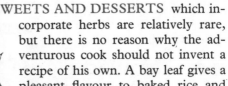 WEETS AND DESSERTS which incorporate herbs are relatively rare, but there is no reason why the adventurous cook should not invent a recipe of his own. A bay leaf gives a pleasant flavour to baked rice and other milk puddings. Herb sugars, made by pounding fresh leaves with granulated sugar, give a subtle fragrance to cakes and puddings. Herb sugars for the store cupboard can also be made by placing a few fresh leaves of, for instance, mint or lemon thyme in a jar of sugar and leaving for about 2 weeks, stirring occasionally. Several herbs are good with fruit; try rosemary, basil or mint with fruit salads and in jams and jellies.

SWEET BASIL OMELETTE

2 eggs   *butter*
2 leaves sweet basil   *lemon juice*
2 dessertspoons sugar

Pound the basil with half the sugar into a fine, pale green aromatic powder. Separate the eggs and beat the whites until stiff. Beat the yolks lightly with the rest of the sugar and fold gently into the whites.

Heat a small piece of butter in the omelette pan, pour in the egg mixture and cook gently until the omelette is just setting, with the top still moist and fluffy. Slide on to a warm plate without folding, sprinkle with the basil sugar and a few drops of lemon juice.

PINEAPPLE AND MINT

This unusual sweet makes an attractive party centrepiece. Slice the leafy top off a large ripe pineapple, using a sharp stainless steel knife. Scoop out the flesh, leaving the rind intact and about half an inch of flesh all round. Dice the flesh, add sugar only if necessary and sprinkle with kirsch or cointreau. Mix in a dozen small mint leaves and chill for an hour.

Pack the chilled pineapple flesh with the mint leaves into the pineapple shell and replace the top. Place in the refrigerator until ready to serve.

Printing and binding by
JOHN BARTHOLOMEW & SON LTD, EDINBURGH
GREAT BRITAIN

41-345-9